A LITTLE BOOK
OF LIVING
THROUGH THE DAY

A Little Book of Living Through the Day
Poems During a Pandemic

David Breeden

Wising Up Press

Wising Up Press
P.O. Box 2122
Decatur, GA 30031-2122
www.universaltable.org

Copyright © 2022 by David Breeden

All rights reserved. No part of this book may be used or reproduced in any manner whatsoever without written permission, except in the case of brief quotations embodied in critical articles or reviews.

ISBN: 978-1-7376940-1-4

Catalogue-in-Publication data is on file with the Library of Congress.
LCCN: 2022936674

For the people who helped us through

Contents

FOREWORD 1
A Little Book of Living Through the Day 3

ONE: ACTS OF COURAGE
Stuck At Times 6
Post Something 8
The Trauma Lasts and 9
Blood For All That 10
Some Things 11
Beautiful Wound, Really 12
This Road To 14
Your Cue 15
Here Is Your Way 16
Fools That We Are 17
Transgressing When I Was a Child 18
About It All 19
Stories Where We Might 20
Rise Against the Lies 21
A Little Address to Humankind 22
Aw Shucks Litany 23
Crèche Like Me 24
Unthinkable Thought 26
Do Ing 27
Say Your Truth 28
The No Thank You Litany 29
Waterloo Up the Road 30
Poetry is Doing 31
Your Castle 32

TWO: THE INMOST FORM
Embodied 34
On Loss 35
Pentecostal Preacher of My Youth 36
Sublime 37

THE LAW OF RECURRENCE	38
EVEN IN DREAMING	39
WRITING PROMPT	40
YOU DO SEE	41
FACE UP, FACE DOWN	42
LAST TRIP OUT	43
ON THE REMOVAL OF A STATUE, ATLANTA, GA	44
2020 SUMMER	45
CHOPPING ON THROUGH	46
FREEDOM ON ITS WAY	47
THE ANCESTORS	48
SENSELESS	50
PERSONAL PRIMORDIAL DAWNS	51
PICK UP THE PHONE	52
TO BE IMPERFECT	54
ATTACHING	56
WIRED FOR THE MOMENT	57
JUST TO START	58
ONLY WILL I REAP: THE SELFISH SONG	60
SING AGAIN	62

THREE: THE TASK OF ART

HERE'S WHERE YOU TRUST ME	64
FLIGHT PATH	65
REMEMBERING A PHOTOGRAPH	66
HANGING A SWING	67
HEAR WHILE YOU'RE HERE	68
GONE . . .	69
FOR SOME OF US, RELIGION	70
HELD, EVEN US	72
OUTSIDE THE STADIUM	73
JUSTICE	74
WELCOME—STEP UP!	75
WHOLE (SORT OF)	76
BEING	77
ANOTHER MAP	78
YOUR PROJECT	79
WE ARE HERE AS IF	80

DARKNESS WITH	81
SMALLER AGAIN	82
ROOM FOR WAITING	83
GRATITUDE	84
ACKNOWLEDGMENTS	86
ABOUT THE AUTHOR	87

FOREWORD

The poems collected here are a result of the pandemic. I wrote them in order to make it through the day, the night, and the day-after-day of the pandemic. Days of worry. Days of confusion. Days of social unrest. Days of figuring out how to get through the days.

I grew up on a farm just east of the Mississippi and north of the Ohio Rivers. I am a farmer from the lower-Midwest with roots in North Carolina. I grew up listening to the Grand Ol' Opry. My rural roots are a through-line of my life. When I look at nature, I can't see only beauty.

Nowadays, I live in a condo in Minneapolis, Minnesota. How I got here both baffles me and fills me with gratitude. I am the senior minister of a historically humanist Unitarian Universalist congregation. Perhaps some of the poems in this collection will sound like liturgy to your ear. That's because they probably are, written for oral presentation in the congregation and at protests.

The pandemic hit congregations hard—we could not do one of the most important things congregations do: gather together. As a minister, I preached not to a gathering of human beings but to a camera. I knew that each person was, like me, living with the day-after-day. What could be said to help us make it?

I officiated weddings and funerals over the months, speaking to the dying and the grieving online. And, every Sunday, I said something to the silence that was the listening congregation.

Many of my ministerial colleagues despaired at preaching to a camera. But as a poet, I am accustomed to speaking to silence. Not to no one, mind you. But silent and imagined faces.

What words might reassure after hours of "doom-scrolling"? Might reassure but not lie?

For us all, the pandemic has been a time to make use of our inner resources. For me, my most dependable inner resource is writing these poems that have added up to a little book about living through the day.

May they help you do that as well.

A Little Book of Living Through the Day

This is a little book about
living through the day. It's
not much about more, but

not much more stays, and
not much more is true than
that you, dear one, make it

through today, this day, of
stasis, disaster, wonder,
boredom, death, and love.

I gathered these words,
hugged them together,
during a great plague
that I lived through.
Perhaps you did, too.

ONE

ACTS OF COURAGE

What this world needs is truth, not consolation.
 ~Jean-Luc Nancy, *Hegel: The Restlessness Of The Negative*

Sometimes even to live is an act of courage.
 ~Lucius Annaeus Seneca

Stuck At Times

Remember: you can live through
the stasis of the afternoon.

I've been there.
You've been there.
We've seen it,

> the mottled window panes
> clotted in finger prints,
> the leaves of ornamental
> trees stillborn in the air.

The stasis of the afternoon
can be survived, whatever
time it arrives.

You've done it.
I've done it.
We've seen it.

> Sometimes it is a chair.
> Sometimes it is a bed.
> Sometimes only the dirt.

> Wherever. We have survived
> the stasis of the afternoon,

by throwing our hearts against
the egregious door;
by writing into the air.

Whichever. Whatever.
All of the above.

      You've done it.
      I've done it.

We have survived
the stasis of
the afternoon.

Post Something

I tell myself to see things
—in my mind I mean—
as they really happened,
not as I've said out loud,
not as I've wished them.
I tell myself to see things

as they were—the curve
to the road, the trees as
they unfolded. I tell myself
to see everything just as
it really was. The trees.

The lane. The light sudden.
I look to see things as
they were, not as I have
said so many times aloud.
Not as I have wished them
to be. I tell myself to see

things there as they were.
Not as I have remembered.
Not as I have said they were.
Not as I have said aloud.
I tell myself. I cannot hear.

The Trauma Lasts and

I hear it. Or
think I do. The
unbearable

above you.
Around. Until
nothing was

at all but fear.
I feel it. I think
I do. Or only

wish I could to
take some hurt
away. It was

your address.
Where you
lived. Almost

survived. Nearly.
Though no one
lives really after

that.

Blood For All That

Let's just say it pours
out of me sometimes.
The words, I mean. I

know it cost Odin a lot.
A spear in his side for
the runes to fall out.

Sorry. I really am. That
my words are not like
that. Perhaps. Maybe

they are not etched in
stone. Carved in rock.
Yet, if you want to see,

here it is—my blood,
just the same for that.

S̲ome T̲hings

Like crumpled
brown leaves,
some things

won't be said,
not even in
scrawls.

Some things.
Love. Death.
Afternoons.

This or that.
Or holding on

like crumpled
brown leaves.

Beautiful Wound, Really

It comes out of nowhere—
out of the forever that
locks the soul and throws
the key into one abyss or
another. It comes of
having an umbilical cord.

It turns us to shadows
on the heath, howling
at the dark, complaining

of the local musicians.
It looks like boredom
sometimes; sometimes

despair, sometimes
voiceless, panicked
terror—or all—it's

hard to tell when
you aren't
breathing.

It is the wound
that makes you
rise and shine.

That leaves you
staring out windows.
That leaves you

spelunking.
That corners
your songs.

It's the rip in
the fabric of
your only

space and time.
It comes of belly
buttons and leaves . . .

never. It's what
you're holding on-
to with every song.

This Road To

I've been on that road.
That road you know.
That road to nowhere.

Been there. Been that
cliché. Look. Look up
from the handlebars.

You are on this road.
You know this road.
Road to everywhere.

Your Cue

There's a fanfare playing.
It's big and grand. There's
a fanfare will play until you

go get those flowers. Go.
That's your cue. Go on
out and take that bow. You

have been living for this
even though you have
not. Go on. Take that

bouquet. It's your gold
watch. No chain. Nothing
like commitment. Take

it. Go. That is your cue.
The fanfare is playing.
Go on out and take a bow.

Here Is Your Way

You know that place.
That place you get
off the highway. Yes.

That's the place
you will respect,
or not, according

to who you are.
That is a dark place.
I get that, but yet

it is your mile
marker. Your place
to be. Go off

there. Trust the
darkness. Love it,
until it is your way.

Fools That We Are

You will tell your
story of humanity
and who it was
when you knew

a thing or two.
You will tell your
story of how it

was and who it
was and your
story of being
human as you

happened to be.
You will tell your
story. And the

ape will tell hers.
We will tell our
stories. Together
as it must be.

Or another way,
fools that we are.

Transgressing When I Was a Child

I loved it when the cigarettes
came into the house. Forbidden

as it was any other time but
when my aunt and uncle came

>   our way. To stay the night for
>   whatever reason we all made up.
>   I loved it. The transgressive

cigarettes saying there was
something else there. Another

way of being. Never did I
understand what it is *that* said,

>   yet I loved it, the the cigarettes
>   transgressing when I was a child.

About It All

What more might there
be to say to say everything
there is to say about it

all? Anything more?
After all, there have

been people here and all.
Others on the journey
of what it's meant to be

human here on the world.
What more might there

be to do after everything
that has been done in
the world? So much.

So much more to be
done upon this world.

Stories Where We Might

How how many times
have we tried to write
ourselves into myth?

And as many times,
we failed. No, none
will scramble into myth—

it's a sheer rock face.
But story is another
thing. A way to drive

the pegs that being hangs
its hat on. From there
we can be what is,

living into being only us
chickens here. In a coop,
perhaps. Or a yard.

Or the free birds we
have dreamed of. No,
not a one of us will

climb into myth, but
—happy day— we all
can swing into a story

everyone understands.

Rise Against the Lies

Wince. Wince again. Still, the fog is there.
Still the whistling wind that never stills.

Here's to our failure to think clearly. Ever.
Here's to thinking that we do. Too often.

Here's to how truth seeps in. Slowly. Cheers!
(Or guffaws. Snickers. Boos. Whatever.)

Here's to the pieces we call "put together."
Here's to the fragments in scattered pieces.

Here's to the motions we call living.
Here's to the moments we call "right here."

Let's agree to this much:
that we will not pull away.

Consider how this works: the earth
does not pull away from the sky.
Consider how this works:

the sky does not leave the earth behind.
Here's to a rise against the lies. Cheers!

And to so much more.
Cheers. Truly. *A ta santé*

A Little Address to Humankind

There will be a sunrise
with or without us, we
see, waking up to dawn.

There's no bad weather,
some folks say, only
bad clothes. See that

from inside or
from out. Or both.

Aw Shucks Litany

Put your hands
in any pockets
you've got. "Aw,

shucks," you say.
"Doesn't have to
be this way. Can

be another way,"
you say. A way where
there's no shade on

our acts and all we
say is "aw, shucks."
Seriously. It can be

another way. A way
where we don't put
any shade on any acts.

Where it's OK to say
it can be another way.
Where all there is to

say is "aw shucks."

CRÈCHE LIKE ME

So many figures
dark in a box,
faces I studied,
each hand-painted
expression. "Made
in Japan." The
sweep of a brush
of artists long dead.

Faces in a dark
box. I don't know
where. Far away.

Can't be opened.
Won't be opened.
Perhaps not even
there. I gathered
them, saving my

dimes, 1960s.
Chalk figures
for a quarter, I
remember each
expression, detail—

Jesus, Mary, Joseph
with a wire for a cane.
Shepherd. Wise men.
Sheep with legs too
thin to stand. That
gray donkey. Gone,
the collecting. The
endless rearranging.
The angel in pink.

Gone. Perhaps dark
in a box somewhere.

Perhaps long broken.
Dare I say it: Like me.

UNTHINKABLE THOUGHT

There you go, calling it
a weed and unthinkable.

Here it is, come to that,
thinkable and reborn,

saying all the while,
"Deal with it. I'm here."

Yet, there it is—
the unthinkable

thought out loud
and as solid as

cold asphalt.

Do Ing

Makin' do is
what you do
when nothin'
else is workin'
for you . . . .

Makin' do is
what you do
when nothin'
ain't workin,'
like most of
the time, for
most of us.

Makin' do is
all there is to
do when most
of life is
happenin'.

Makin' do is
what you do
if your life is
like most of us.

Say Your Truth

Lotsa people say
It ain't that way

Lotsa people say
It ain't that way

Lotsa people say
It ain't that way

Doesn't matter what
lotsa people say

Doesn't matter what
lotsa people say

Doesn't matter what
lotsa people say

We know it's
just this way

We know it's
just this way

We know it's
just this way

No matter what
lotsa people say

The No Thank You Litany

Yes, this is what they're going to tell you.
Here's what they are going to tell you.
They're going to tell you you need this
because this is what everyone has.

Here's what you're going to tell them.
This is what you're going to tell them—
this is what I've got
and this is all I need.

They are selling the old stuff.
Listen to them selling the old stuff.
All we who know can say,
all we who know can only say—

No, thank you. All we can do
is say it polite: No thank you!

Yes, they will weep and wail.
Listen to them weep and wail.
Because they told you what
you need and you said . . .

no thank you.

Waterloo Up the Road

What do you do
when Waterloo
is right up
the road?

(Because Waterloo,
as you know,
is always
right up the road.)

Waiting.

What do you do,
when it occurs to you
that Waterloo
is right up the road?

Waiting.

You keep in step;
that's what you do;
you step up the road
to the Waterloo

waiting. Coldly.

You walk on;
that's what you do
when Waterloo is
always up the road.

Poetry is Doing

Poetry is doing
in the face of
nothing. That's

why I'm thinking
of writing my
life these days.

Perhaps to find
a rhythm, somehow,
to my days. Maybe,

somehow, to make
sense of bad moves,
of swerves into muddy

ditches. Where is
it? I ask the shadow.
What is it that drove

the insanity
on? Poetry is
doing in the

face of
nothing.

Your Castle

See this, see this
as it is,
   or at least as
you need it
   to be.

        A stone?
        A stick?
        A glass slipper?

See it.
See it.

   This. Here.
What you need
   it to be.

TWO

THE INMOST FORM

Mistrust is the intelligence of the disadvantaged.
 ~Peter Sloterdijk

I strove to seize the inmost form
With ardor fierce and hands of flame
 ~William Blake, "The Chrystal Cabinet"

Embodied

A.

What is there
  to say
    but in
    speaking?
What there is
  to say?

B.

Not in the mind
but in the words
      in the speaking
      aloud to the others
that we find
what it is to say

On Loss

One foot
    in front
then the other.

It's all and
    only
about going on.

That road
    behind;
that gone time

is good and
    done.
The road

ahead.
    One foot,
then another.

Pentecostal Preacher of My Youth

Brother Van was
An uneducated man
Coal miner at twelve
Shot for striking
And left for dead

Saw Jesus there
Bleeding in the weeds
Brother Van knew
What he had to do
Go preach Christ
And him crucified

Brother Van could
Preach with a glance
Pray up a sweat
Convict with a word
Heal with a touch

Brother Van didn't
Die after gettin' shot
And very nearly bleedin'
Plumb to death so
He preached Christ
And him crucified.

Sublime

Somewhere. Somewhere
is the moment
      when the trees sway
      and the leaves fall.
That is the sublime,
 waiting to be held
  for the moment,
   this moment
      when the trees sway
      and the leaves fall
until they are
shining images
folded into a book.

The Law of Recurrence

The big bad
  Wolf
Is always
  @ the door

Knocking, knocking
  Always
@ the door

  Sometimes
A house of straw
  Sometimes wood

And you know the rest
For there's no rest

This always
  @ the door

Knocking, knocking

Even in Dreaming

You are not there,
        never were, not
        even in dreams.
The stones you've

traced, the mortar,
        is not there,
even in dreams.

Those walls, the
        wire and barbs,
        are not there,
even in dreams.

Writing Prompt

The prompt says to
gather papers from
your mother's life

and tell a story.
That's easy—she

left a driver's license,
social security card.
Unsigned.

People who can't
read, who can't
write, leave few

words behind. Go
ahead, follow the
trail. It leads to the

oblivion left in the
wake of the poor.
Unsigned.

You Do See

You do understand that
I don't understand. Let's
start there. For me the
yellowed light in a tiny

parking lot is enough.
Whatever goes on there
looks warm to me. I

want to pull in. Park. See
what's on offer in that
warmth. Yes, I see snow
beginning to fall. Yes

I understand the cold.
I understand how large
the dark is that surrounds.

Face Up, Face Down

Let's face it: even
whirling dervishes
get stuck in traffic

in this world.
Sucks to be us,

in that way. Makes
some insufferable.
Serious. Programmatic.

After all, look at
what we have
to work with—

A bit of everything,
Not all of anything,
most likely. Small

chance. As the jack-
boots of partiality
keep stomping by.

Last Trip Out

The earth there is driven flat
by wind, rain, and mowing.

I didn't want to leave you there.

>We've left together,
>time after time, leaving
>those we loved one by one.

Yet just like any flower
plucked, there's always a last one,

isn't there? Am I right about that?
One last trip out.

On the Removal of a Statue, Atlanta, GA

Metal man, keep your chin up.
Metal man, show your face.
Metal man, face the consequences
of the flesh you led
to their insensate deaths.

Man of copper and tin
on your high horse, lying
bald-faced to the world.
Man of copper and tin,
ride your shame down into
the heartless grave you dug.

Metal man, you lied;
metal man, you lie still;
metal man, frozen in guilt.
Metal man frozen in shame,
high and mighty on your
horse of tin and copper
leading tender flesh on
to insensate deaths.

Stiff bronze lip, metal man.
Stiff traitor's gait, metal man.

You rode into eternal
shame, fool in metal.

2020 Summer

Words and violence,
violence and words.

In the late night dark,
broken glass, silence.

Silence that asks us to
throw words into it,

meaning. Stories
onto the night.

We animals who create
symbols and cover them

with meanings—like
graffiti on railroad cars

passing like nights,
too fast to read.

In the dark of early hours,
breaking glass, screams.

Anger.
Fear.

Violence we must throw
meaning onto, words.

Stories.

Chopping On Through

That hydra has a lotta heads.
It's pointless to say "too many."
The hydra has a lotta heads, but

no, you cannot say "too many."

No, you can't nuke the beast.
Nope, can't bomb it either.
Tanks won't do.
No.
Or edicts either.
Nope, it's got to be hacked,

one sharp-toothed head at a time,
with a good ol' fashioned edge.

The hydra has a lot of heads.
"Wack-a-Mole," it's easy to say.
"Pointless" rolls off the tongue.
"Let's just leave that beast alone."

No, you can't walk
on down the road.

Hack on in.
You can be brave.
Chop one off.
Sear the stub.

Go for the next—
It's how Hercules did it.
It's called doing your best.

It's called liberation.

Freedom on Its Way

No, you can't redeem
the dust of the ancestors.
They did their musts.
They served their time.

Can't fix 'em.
Can't free 'em.
Can't explain away.

No, you can't redeem
the dust of the ancestors.

There's a thing called "past."
That's a thing called "done."
You can't redeem the dust.

But pull on those boots
and pull up those jeans
anyway. Go out and be
today. Go, help
raise some dust.

The Ancestors

I wrote to my dear Christopher,
brother in the poetry, the moment
I read it in "23 and Me:"

Congolese.
Congolese.

Back in the family past,
not mentioned in my
Southern family even if
anyone alive in my time knew.

Congolese. The Congo.
Who might it have been?
How might it have been?
Long before the war, no doubt,
long before the enslaved were free . . .

did he or she escape?
I'm hoping so.
Who did he or she find
among the poor farmers
to fall in love with?
I so hope it was love.

I so hope it was escape.
Where would the name be?
Who would the name be
if my family had had a bible
to write the names in
or any way to write words?

But, no. Congolese.
It's written in the ancestors.
It's written in the genes.
Lost or buried, I will never know.
Had to get white.
Had to get the gimmes.
Had to grab that privilege
and hide that one drop of . . .
that one drop of . . .
that one drop
the South so fears.

When I read the news
I wrote to my dear friend Christopher,
brother. Proud in the knowledge.
Shamed in the loss.

Senseless

The world will make sense . . .
 if you let it. Life will be logical . . .
if you let it be. Don't you let it.

    Because the world is not logical;
    the world does not make sense.

The violence does not make sense.
The hate does not make sense.
The suffering does not make sense.

    The starvation does not make sense.
    The waste does not make sense.

The world does not make sense.
Don't let it start making sense to you.
Don't let it poison your pure, pure heart,

    to allow sense to seep in. Don't
    let it get to your pure pure heart.

Personal Primordial Dawns

What a shock when we crawl out
of the muck of our personal
primordial dawns to find there

> have been so many matinées
> and soirees for so many.
> What's left to do? we ask

the empty cinema marquee.
Nothing, nothing pipes in
a dusty street through

> the smoke and ash
> of so many lives.

What a shock
to crawl out
of the muck of

> our personal
> primordial dawns.

Pick Up the Phone

Creation stories start
in darkness. Then

something moves.

Sometimes it's sex.
Sometimes breath.

Often it's a god.
Voila! There's us!

Then we are naughty
and things go awry

which is always kind
of good with bad shot

through, all in a clump
like strands of cotton candy,

but hard, like death
and endless forms.

Which brings me to today
when I've bought the wrong

thing for a birthday. And
not bought a bus ticket.

And forgot who knows what
else. Where are the gods

like that? Tired, muddled,
plugging away at a telephone

switchboard like in old movies?
"Hello?" Hello? It's dark.

But that's another movie.
Some other story altogether.

No one. No story.
Nothing's there.

Creation stories.
They don't come

out of nothing.

To Be Imperfect

Oh, my, here I am, my
metaphysics all tangled
up again. Like a root-bound
plant, I'll need another
pot, a more expansive one
this time. To grow into.

Walking on water,
striding between
mountain peaks—
these are the dreams,
yet so few of us
ever see the ground.
The earth between

our toes. Here I am
again, an expression,
unaware. Unaware.
When we talk about the
limitless, isn't that
merely about the yarns

we can knit about
the spillage of
our lives? A grasp
at the sand, the
air that we are.

Who we are.
What we are.
How we are.

We are only as separate
as we think, separate,
though living does
remind us sometimes
that I am not I at all.

Attaching

all our lives are
pick up a pebble
pick up a pebble
pick up a pebble
we love

all our lives are
lose a pebble
lose a pebble
lose a pebble
we love

all our lives are
gain and lose
gain and lose
gain and lose
then lose

all our lives are
the day and night
the day and night
the day and night
and the gray

all our lives we attach
and attach to the things

the ones we learn to love
all our lives we yearn

and yearn for more
as we lose
all that we love

Wired for the Moment

Like the latch on a barn door,
a rusted steel hasp wired together
and inevitably giving way,

there's no easy way out—
that's axiomatic, but out
it is, like the cattle

in that barn—
there is an end,
even to the toil,

even to the travail,
even to the pain,
to the death rattle even.

It does come: an end.

Just To Start

Here's a quandary:
is it this or that?
Yes, there's the old

flip-a-coin thing—
heads 'er lie. If
that's enough, take

it. There are other
ways to choose a
binary. An either / or.

You can choose Yes.
Or you can choose No.
Sure. You can

choose perhaps / . . .
That sort of thing.
But still you're on your . . .

the you in all this, is

a raggedy edge. A
perhaps, really, in one
way to see it. Or an

everything and enough
in another. Let's choose
that one. Just because.

Just because we've
got to start somewhere.
And right here is good.

All enough. Let's pick
right here. And "you're
enough." That's a start.

Only Will I Reap: The Selfish Song

never did i sow
only did i reap

no seedtime for me,
only more, more

I did not stop
to consider

I did not stop
to converse

it was never
seedtime for me

only harvest
only more, more

and reaping, as
I did not sow

no listening, no
because I need the

reward, never
the sweat, no

never did i sow
only did i reap

      the whirlwind
      the wisdom says

      is only
      what i reap

Sing Again

It's a parching wind that
takes the breath away.
It's an acrid smoke that
robs the air, stinging.

It's a slip in stepping
among the drowned stones,
and you are silenced,

the silence of the long dead;
the silence of the never born.
Yet, look. It is a glimmer.

Faint. Still, you might grasp
it—a rising song; a new
seeing. A place to stand.
A way to say the unsaid.

THREE

THE TASK OF ART

To harmonize the whole is the task of art.
~Wassily Kandinsky

I am. I become. I write. I write only in order to become.
~ Edmond Jabès

Here's Where You Trust Me

Here's where you
have to trust me:

You can build a fire.
You can watch it burn.
You can dance in
the joy of the vortex.

You can come down.
You can come home.

Here's where you
really have to trust me:

You can throw on water.
You can throw on kerosene
You can dash around.
You can dither in

the sadness of obligation.
You can run away.

There's no other way.
You have to trust me.

Flight Path

Thin branches wave
with each sparrow
that lands or leaves.

        Perhaps they wonder,
        the sparrows, what
        those slow shadows

are. Tin tubes full
of people flying to
find thin branches.

Remembering a Photograph of My Parents' Lawn

I must say I looked at the roses,
the mowed grass, trimmed trees,
and saw nothing to remark on.
I must say I did not respect how
much in sweat and worry it cost
to raise those walls against chaos.
I must say that I never saw.
Not until years later, after

the roses, the grass, the trimming

had all gone away. No smiling
for a calm photograph. No
pausing for a casual remark.
All gone. All gone, the smiles.
All gone the pride simply in
accomplishing. All gone,
the wrinkles in a face so worn
in worry, yet in that moment

forever triumphant, smiling.

Hanging a Swing

That tree that's planted
in your mind, the one with
the serpent entwined, you
know that's not real,
yet here you are with

that tree in your mind.
Let's not chop it down,
though that's a response.

Let's not chop it down,
but look instead beyond
the serpent and the up
and down. Let's look
around and see the shade

and maybe hang a swing
in that tree and sway
in that tree in your mind.

Hear While You're Here

Listen. Listen, while you're here, to
the grating, the beautiful, human song.
Sure, you may learn animal voices.

    Sure, you may learn the speech of trees.
    Perhaps you may learn to hear the sound
    of your heart before it steps into silence.

        Whatever else you do here, please,
        please, hear the terrifying
        and the gorgeous human song.

GONE . . .

Ain't no candle in the window.
Won't be one no more.

        Walk on in the dark.
        Turn up your collar to the cold.

Ain't no candle in the window.
Won't be one no more.

For Some of Us, Religion

For some of us
religion was never
a game—you're
in or out. The
stakes are all

you've got or
nothing. For
some of us you
are all in—hell
and all. Or out.

For some of us
it's no lark—you're
in or out on all—
It all is inspired,
a god's word, or

not. For some
of us it's all in
or walk away.
For some of us,
here are the chips,

and I see you and
raise. Or not. It's
not a game. It's
in or out. Your
house, your watch.

Pony up for the
heaven or hell or
get the hell out
of the game. For
some of us it's not

about the mystery,
the love or whatever.
For some of us
it's the way it says
or it's not at all.

There's no room
here for those who
are only joking.

Held, Even Us

Pebbles don't dream
of becoming stones, do
they? Do boulders

dream mountainous
dreams? The earth
hugs us all, in our

place, even us, if only
we will hold still. Yet
don't we all know

striving? The pebbles,
the stones, boulders,
mountains? You. Me.

Striving toward being
the one that we are
already. Still. Content.

Yet striving always
to be a better stone,
a calmer mountain?

Do pebbles know they
are loved? Do we know
they know, since we see

how still they are? How
centered in their place?

Outside the Stadium

Bread is for memory.
Circuses to forget.
Bread lines for the streets.

Circuses are circles.
"Give us our daily!" once
we cried. "Give us our

special." And still large
spaces fill with dust.
Bread is the size of

always, like the lips
that plead and cry, "More
bread, more circuses!"

Yes, we cry, "more," to
remember. To forget.

J*ustice*

The clockworks of never
clank, clank—"Next time.

Next time." Endlessly
they chatter: "It's coming.

Right up." The clockworks
say, "This time. Next time.

Some very soon fine day."
The clocks whisper

as they tick, "Never.
Never. Never"

Welcome—Step Up!

Where are *you* in all this?
All this life, I mean.
Where is it you call home?

What is it you're calling
"mine?" Here's hoping
you're all in.

All in because . . . we all
are. Seriously.
Because what

else is there than
all in? Welcome.
You're already all in,

always. This is only about
how you do with being all in.
Join in. Re-alize. Be all in.

Everything—and seriously
I mean everything is
all in. Be. Here. With us.

Whole (Sort Of)

I'm picking up the pieces;
I'm searching for the glue;

I'm gathering the shards up
and making something new.

Something of myself to
start again; something

not as I used to be but
together all the same.

I'm gathering the pieces.
I'm picking up the glue.

BEING

I'm mostly "was,"
with very little "to,"

but hold onto "am"
with both old hands.

Another Map

The bad times now. The better
times next. Keeps us here, yes?

Always, always, the promise—

strange times now. Bad times
ahead. Better times just behind

that curtain there. Just wait.

Your Project

There's a project
your life's got;

for some, it's plain;
for others not.

There's a shape
it all will take;

for some it's awry;
for others straight.

There's a back-story
that shapes our end;

we can call it an evil;
we can make it a friend.

There's a project
your life's got;

find it, do it,
hug your ought.

We Are Here As If

Let's be honest. When
we're on a bus, we want
off. When we're off,
we're waiting for a
bus. Let's be honest

with each other and all
the others. We'd rather be
anywhere else. So. Here
we are. Sharing words

and maybe-ifs which
are already plotted,
these words: It's as if
we're in a room and
everyone's speaking

a language we can't
know. It's as if we are
somewhere far from
the bus we wanted.

Darkness With

I've taken my darkness with me
into every place I've known.

Lovely, lots of them. Painful
a few. But I've taken my dark

with me when I've gone. It's
the companion that I've known.

SMALLER AGAIN

They come back, the old fears.
Won't change a thing, but still
they do. "Make yourself small!"

some thin voice shouts. An
Echo. No, an ache, across so
many years. All those things

that mattered rushing back.
Pain. Fear. Cringing. Hoping
to grow smaller still. To

disappear to prove I'm not
much trouble. Don't take much.
Won't do that thing ever again.

Aren't really there at all . . . They
flood back, the old fears. No
walls stop them. No thoughts.

Only living the fear again, as if,
maybe, this time, it's different.

Room for Waiting

There is the arriving.
There is the going away.
There is the train-siding

with its birds and debris.

How fast a world crumbles.
How slowly one gathers again.

And waiting. And waiting.

There is the falling rain
beating,

beating against windows.

How slowly a world gathers,
if ever one arrives. Yet
something glimmers—both

birds and debris. Rain.
Windows. Trains.
Arriving. Arriving.

GRATITUDE

What to say
at the end
of a perfect day
but thank you,
thank you?

        What to say
        at the end
        of a dreadful day
        but thank you,
        thank you?

What to say
to life, to death,
but thank you,
thank you?

ACKNOWLEDGMENTS

"Room for Waiting," *Autumn Sky Poetry*.

Author's photo by Joe Szurszewski.

ABOUT THE AUTHOR

David Breeden holds an MFA degree from the Iowa Writers' Workshop, a PhD from the Center for Writers at the University of Southern Mississippi, and a Master of Divinity from Meadville Lombard Theological School. He is Senior Minister of the First Unitarian Society of Minneapolis. David serves as chair of the American Humanist Association Center for Education.

BOOKS FROM WISING UP PRESS

FICTION

Only Beautiful & Other Stories
Live Your Life & Other Stories
My Name Is Your Name & Other Stories
Kerry Langan

Germs of Truth
The Philosophical Transactions of Maria van Leeuwenhoek
Visible Signs
Heather Tosteson

Not Native: Short Stories of Immigrant Life in an In-Between World
Murali Kamma

Something Like Hope & Other Stories
William Cass

MEMOIR

Journeys with a Thousand Heroes: A Child Oncologist's Story
John Graham-Pole

Keys to the Kingdom: Reflections on Music and the Mind
Kathleen L. Housley

Last Flight Out: Living, Loving & Leaving
Phyllis A. Langton

Green Card & Other Essays
Áine Greaney

POETRY

Source Notes: Seventh Decade
Heather Tosteson

A Hymn that Meanders
Maria Nazos

Epiphanies
Kathleen L. Housley

PLAYS

Trucker Rhapsody & Other Plays
Toni Press-Coffman

WISING UP ANTHOLOGIES

ILLNESS & GRACE: TERROR & TRANSFORMATION

FAMILIES: *The Frontline of Pluralism*

LOVE AFTER 70

DOUBLE LIVES, REINVENTION & THOSE WE LEAVE BEHIND

VIEW FROM THE BED: VIEW FROM THE BEDSIDE

SHIFTING BALANCE SHEETS:
Women's Stories of Naturalized Citizenship & Cultural Attachment

COMPLEX ALLEGIANCES:
Constellations of Immigration, Citizenship & Belonging

DARING TO REPAIR: *What Is It, Who Does It & Why?*

CONNECTED: *What Remains As We All Change*

CREATIVITY & CONSTRAINT

SIBLINGS: *Our First Macrocosm*

THE KINDNESS OF STRANGERS

SURPRISED BY JOY

CROSSING CLASS: *The Invisible Wall*

RE-CREATING OUR COMMON CHORD

GOODNESS

FLIP SIDES:
Truth, Fair Play & Other Myths We Choose to Live By: Spot Cleaning Our Dirty Laundry

ADULT CHILDREN:
Being One, Having One & What Goes In-Between

WISING UP LISTENING PROJECTS

GOD SPEAKS MY LANGUAGE, CAN YOU?
Spiritual Journeys Across Faith Traditions

SHARING THE BURDEN OF REPAIR:
R̲e̲-E̲ntry A̲fter M̲ass I̲ncarceration

Learn more about Universal Table/Wising Up Press:
www.universaltable.org
wisingup@universaltable.org
P.O. Box 2122, Decatur, GA 30031-2122

www.ingramcontent.com/pod-product-compliance
Lightning Source LLC
Chambersburg PA
CBHW022117090426
42743CB00008B/890